PURB
COASTAL
W·A·L·K·S

Rodney Legg

This selection from Rodney Legg's acclaimed series of circular country walks, a model of their kind, comes from the popular publications *Dorset County Magazine* and *Dorset Life*. They now appear in Dorset's first all-colour magazine — *Dorset: The Magazine For People Who Like To Explore.*

dpc

DORSET PUBLISHING COMPANY
at the WINCANTON PRESS   NATIONAL SCHOOL
NORTH STREET   WINCANTON   SOMERSET   BA9 9AT

For **John and Rosemary Palmer**
who have already done them all

Routes are described as found at the time
the walk was researched. All paths are liable
to changes — from both natural
causes and legal diversion. Any
obstructions or other difficulties should be
reported to the local highway authority.
Contact the Rights of Way Office,
Transportation and Engineering Department,
County Hall, Dorchester, Dorset DT1 1XJ.
(01-305-251-000)

Publishing details
First published 1995. Copyright Rodney Legg © 1995
Published by Dorset Publishing Company at the Wincanton Press, National School, North
Street, Wincanton, Somerset BA9 9AT (01-963-325-83) to whom updatings may be sent,
addressed to the author. Distribution in Dorset undertaken by Maurice Hann of the Dorset
Publishing Company from 36 Langdon Road, Parkstone, Poole, Dorset BH14 9EH
(01-202-738-248).

Printing credits
Typeset by Maurice Hann. Printed in Somerset by Cedric Chivers Limited, 9a/9b
Aldermoor Way, Longwell Green, Bristol BS15 7DA (01-179-352-617).

International standard book number
ISBN 0 902129 63 5

Contents

Durdle Door
& White Nothe

The white cliffs of Dorset from Ringstead to Lulworth are strung out along this ten mile walk. It begins from neither honeypot, however, but is based instead on the hamlet of East Chaldon which is still in the back of beyond and feels a million miles away from the holiday coast. From here it is just about possible to walk across the downs, selecting a zig-zag course along four different cross-country rights of way, to reach the cliff path without having come closer than a hundred yards to a caravan or car. On the coast the instant objective is Durdle Door, but to see it from the west rather than the customary viewing platform on the other side.

Durdle Door is the tall rock arch of upturned Portland stone at the west of a bastion of these hard rocks that have partially kept the sea from breaking through into the softer chalk behind. Breaches have been made either side and, of course, through it. The arch is open to the south-westerlies and a little bay is developing on the landward side, between it and the chalk cliffs of Newlands Warren.

"Durdle" is pure Dorset dialect on Saxon roots. William Barnes should have made something of it as one of the best examples to be found on the Ordnance map, for its name is derived from the Old English "thyrel" or "thirl" which means holed; initial "th" sounds being pronounced "d" in the Dorset dialect.

The finest single feature on the chalk cliffs does not even carry a name on the map though it is known locally as Fountain Rock. Seaward of a couple of concrete obelisks, between White Nothe and West Bottom, stands a vertical column of chalk that is three hundred feet high. Though joined to the cliff on the north side, it is rounded to the south as a perfect semi-circle. There is a pebble beach below. Those obelisks above are two slender concrete-faced pyramids, twenty feet high, which stand on the grassy slopes above West Bottom at about 510 feet and 540 feet above sea level. They are set as sea marks which, when lined up, show the safe approach to Portland harbour from the south. The passage they pinpoint is from south-by-south-west to north-by-north-cast; charting a course between the perilous ledges off Portland Bill and the parlous offshore Shambles sandbank. It comes to life as a sea-lane when a Royal Navy carrier group, such as *Ark Royal* with her escort frigates, sails up-Channel and turns to port off Portland Bill to come into Dorset waters in single file a mile or so east of Portland.

Former coastguard cottages on the top of White Nothe, at 495 feet above sea level, are the highest inhabited buildings on the Dorset coast. Indeed, they must be contenders for that superlative for a good deal of the rest of the English coast.

Among those who has enthused over this uplifting panorama was Dorset essayist Llewelyn Powys who died in 1939 and whose gravestone is close to the upper obelisk on the slope above West Bottom. He always insisted that correctly the headland was White Nose — because, as he rightly pointed out, that is its shape. It is, however, a losing battle these days since the advent of a string of direction markers with "White Nothe" literally cut in stone. His brother, Theodore Powys, also wrote in these hills but his obsession was with people rather than topography. The walk passes Beth Car, the red-brick villa set back from the south side of the lane at the west end of East Chaldon, where he lived from about 1910 to 1940. Instead of trying to change the names on the skyline Theodore invented his own and one has stuck to this day. "Madder Hill," on the other side of the lane, provided the view and solitude that he found vital for his work.

Rosemary Manning stimulated the Powys revival, calling *Mr Weston's Good Wine* "one of the few perfect novels in the English language," and it was then re-issued as a Penguin classic. It tells how God visited East Chaldon, or "Folly Down" as it is called, in the person of Mr Weston, a travelling wine merchant, who came in an old Ford van.

Theodore deserted Beth Car for the mid-Dorset village of Mappowder when the Dorset coast became an armed camp and German invasion threatened. In 1953 he died and though his output rated an obituary in *The Times* it was to denigrate the creations for which he is now acclaimed. He was accused of degrading "the rich comedy of which he was capable to an almost bestial farce". A more balanced view is to consider that he penned delightful allegories on the inherent contradiction between an ever-present God and nature's obsession with procreation. "Queer, blind, half-dumb, earthy folk, lusting and fumbling in the endless preoccupation of sex," was how one critic summed up Powys's characters.

They were the fellow inhabitants of his village of life. I met one. "You going to leave that car there?" a contemporary village person asked with a grimace. That look kept returning to me as recent re-readings of Theodore Powys spilled back into my mind. He can prepare you for much worse encounters. It does lessen one's curiosity for looking into any of the old farm buildings or even behind the gorse bushes on the downs. May you be spared the occasional native stepping from the page.

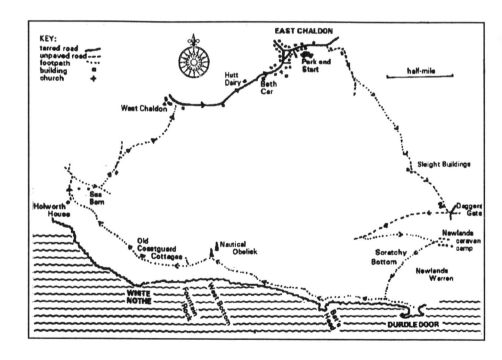

● Turn south from the A352 at the Red Lion and drive through Winfrith Newburgh. Turn right at the parish church and drive into the hamlet of East Chaldon in a mile. Park at the side of the lane, making sure that you do not obstruct any farm entrances. (Ordnance Survey map reference SY 793 833.)

● Walk back the way that you have come, eastwards out of the village in the direction of Winfrith Newburgh, and pass the farm, Dairy House, and roadside sewage plant. Then, in a hundred yards, turn right at the bend and walk uphill along a gritty track signed: "Bridleway Daggers Gate 1". It turns left above the bungalow and then continues straight ahead at the next house, down and around the corner. The farm track meanders up a long valley but you leave it in 450 yards. This is at a point about 150 yards after the second gate, where you fork left through a gate set into the hedge which runs to the left of the main track.

● On the other side of the gate you continue straight ahead, now keeping the same hedgerow to your right. Continue up the valley towards Sleight Buildings, which are on the horizon and nearly a mile away. To reach these barns you go through a pair of gates and then climb out of the valley through a third gate. Pass the chalkpit and walk up to the top end of the sheep-down where you go through the upper of the two metal gates.

● Follow the farm track which skirts to the left of the main barn and then continue up the hill. This farm road brings you to another pair of barns and then down towards the tarred road at Daggers Gate. Fifty yards before reaching the road you instead turn right. Turn on to the second farm track which runs beside a hedgerow. It is signed: "Ringstead 4, White Nothe 2½." Follow this up and over the hill, heading for the main entrance to Portland harbour. As the full outline of Portland becomes visible you approach a stile but do not cross it.

● Here, instead, you turn sharply left. Put your back to the stile and walk away from it in the direction of Newlands Farm Camp Site. This soon becomes evident in half a mile. At first you are heading towards the outline of Bindon Hill, the unspoilt military skyline to the left of the caravans. Then the path follows the right hand fence and drops to a chalky track in the valley floor.

● Turn right along this track, continuing downhill and with your back to the caravans. Then the path goes through a gate and follows the fence, which is immediately to your right, around the slope of Newlands Warren and into Scratchy Bottom. At the end you'll soon see Durdle Door, from three hundred yards, but if you are itching for a closer encounter you can turn left along the cliff path. It is inadvisable to try your luck getting down on the beach at this point!

● Our route, on the other hand, is up to the right over Swyre Head and Bat's Head. It is signed: "Ringstead 3½, White Nothe 2." Bat's Head is pierced with Bat's Hole; a pocket-size sea-cut arch. Keep on the cliff path. In a mile, above the precipitous Fountain Rock, you pass below the lower of two obelisks which are a nautical alignment to show the southern approach into Portland harbour. Continue to White Nothe, passing the former coastguard cottages. Follow the path immediately above the undercliff ("Weymouth 7, Ringstead 1½") which descends gradually at first to the grounds of Holworth House which is a mile away in the trees.

● Here you turn right, leaving the arrows and signs of the coast path and instead walk northwards up the drive — straight inland. In a hundred yards you come to a junction of tracks and turn right, continuing uphill. In another two hundred yards, just after the postbox, you come to a bend. Turn right here, across the stile to the left of the gate. The path is signed: "West Lulworth 5. No cars please." It passes the thatched Sea Barn, National Trust owned, and then goes through another gate.

● In a hundred yards between the barn and the hilltop there is a gate on the left, shortly before another gate and stile combination. Turn left at the first gate; once again northward and inland. The track is arrowed: "West Chaldon 1." It climbs a rise, passes an asbestos barn and continues as a farm road beside an arable field. Two hundred yards after the asbestos barn you fork right, leaving the main track and striking off into the field. Walk diagonally across it, heading for the third electricity pole (counting to the right from the track). You are heading towards the skyline that is just to the right of the grassy tump which is Theodore Powys's "factional" Madder Hill. Go through an iron gate, to the right of the rooftops of West Chaldon farmstead, and descend to the next gate.

● From here you drop down to the tarred road and turn right. Pass cottages numbers 28 and 27. Next, in a quarter of a mile, are numbers 26 and 25, which are also semi-detached in matching bands of flint and brick. Then comes "Chaldon Herring (East Chaldon)" with the pseudo-old Hutt Dairy on the left and Beth Car, Theodore Powys's red-brick house, next on the right. The village proper starts with the Old Vicarage, a busy rookery, the church and Manor House. Fork right at the village green and then turn right to find your car.

Lulworth Cove & Durdle Door

There is no shortage of classic textbook geology on this six mile walk which is at the heart of Dorset's holiday coast. It starts from the end of the B3070 at Lulworth Cove where the sea has breached the hard limestone barrier of the outer cliffs and scooped out a semi-landlocked bay of tennis-bat shape.

Its encroachment at this point was aided by a small stream and the soft, coloured Wealden sands and clays that lie between the hard Purbeck rocks facing the English Channel and the line of chalk hills behind.

To know more, you have only to stand at Stair Hole which is the principal setting for the West Lulworth geology lesson. The bowl-shaped depression above the rocks can act as a soundbox and at any time of the year you are liable to hear a teacher shouting its meaning at his impatient herd.

Basically it goes like this. Lulworth is the best example in Britain of different rates of coastal erosion. Further to the west is the magnificent sea-arch of Durdle Door.

At Stair Hole there is a gash and another sea-arch where the waves are breaking through the limestone to gouge out a second Lulworth Cove. The rocks themselves display tilted and twisted strata where movement of the harder Portland stone rucked up the Middle and Upper Purbeck beds. This is called the Lulworth Crumple and is another of the classic landforms on the learning menu.

It all makes for superb scenery. For almost a century the Cove received regular summertime visits from shallow-draught paddle steamers operating from Weymouth, Swanage and Bournemouth, which came right in to a landing stage of planking that extended from beside the outlet of the stream.

Shell fish used to be caught on some scale. There was an oyster pond on the west side of the Cove, constructed among the rocks at the low-tide mark, where fishermen kept their catches until they were wanted for market. On Easter Monday a waterside fair used to be held there.

It is the spot where the poet John Keats apparently spent his last hours on English soil, when the *Maria Crowther* put in whilst en route for Italy, on 30 September 1820. It was during this brief Dorset interlude, whilst Captain Walsh waited for favourable wind, that he is said to have written his final poem, the sonnet "Bright star, would I were steadfast as thou art".

The walk escapes into the hills for the landward side of the circuit, on to unspoilt chalk downland of bell-flowers, knapweed and butterflies, and the paddocks at the back of the village. Even on busy days, Lulworth has an empty hinterland.

Traffic in the village mars but has not destroyed a fine collection of thatch and quaint corners that manage still to be rustic.

There is also a splendid bucolic aside, for en route you pass the former inn which was visited by a king, searching out the real-life family that had provided the prototype for one of his favourite characters on the London stage.

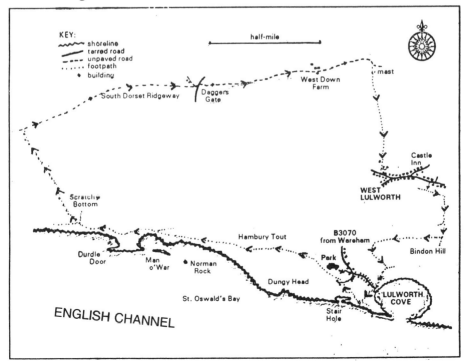

• Park in the main car park at Lulworth Cove (Ordnance Survey map reference SY 822 801). Walk back to the turning circle at the car park entrance, beside the Lulworth Cove Hotel, and go straight over into the almost picturesque lane that leads to the Cove itself.

• Turn right at the shingle beach, crossing the stream, and then immediately right beside the slipway of Lulworth Marine. Walk up the flight of steps and then uphill to the coastal viewpoint. From it, on one side look back at the cove and on the other down into the dramatic mini-cove behind Stair Hole.

• At the end of the open space you cross a drive and then the car park. This time you leave it at the pair of stiles on the far side and climb the chalky path up and over Hambury Tout. You are now on the cliff path, above St Oswald's Bay, with the Norman Rock offshore to your left and a line of lesser navigation hazards stretching across to the Man o' War Cove and the open sea.

• Next is the Durdle Door projection of even lumpier rock, still joined to the mainland by a hazardous causeway. Then, a mile from the car park, you have the famous view of the rock-arch itself.

• Follow the cliff path for a further 400 yards. After a short climb you drop into a deep gully with a steep slope directly ahead of you.

• This is almost your lucky day! Instead of that stiff climb you turn right at the second stile, diagonally up the slope up the gentler signed path marked "Footpath, The Warren".

• The path, for half a mile, climbs the downland pasture above Scratchy Bottom as you head inland, across the sheep slopes. At the top, with your back to both Durdle Door and Scratchy Bottom, you come to a fence-line with a stile and a pointer to "The Warren, White Nothe".

• Cross it and turn right, following the fence uphill to another stile, beside the gate in 40 yards. Continue to follow the fence in this field, into the corner in 200 yards.

• Turn right through the gate and walk straight ahead along this track, which is the south

Dorset Ridgeway, for a mile. Keep following the fence-line, avoiding offshooting paths.

● The main track brings you down to a grain store, machinery barn and the tarred road at Daggers Gate.

● Turn left for just ten yards and then right, up the gravel track to West Down Farm which is also signed "Burngate 1½".

● You come to the farm in half a mile. Continue straight ahead along the main track. In another 400 yards, after passing through the hedgerow on the skyline, this farm road bends to the left and brings you to a pole that acts as a television mast.

● Turn right here, keeping the mast and its hedge to your left, and head straight downhill towards the sea. As you descend from the ridge the village of West Lulworth comes into view. The last section of path into the village is through a narrow belt of woodland between houses and bungalows.

● Continue straight ahead, down to the tarred road opposite Fremar and No. 4.

● Turn left along West Road for a hundred yards, to the junction with the main street. The last building on the left before the Cornish granite war memorial is Churchfield House. This was the Red Lion Inn, visited by King George III in 1802, where Irish playwright John O'Keeffe had found innkeeper William Randall whom he immortalised as John Barleycorn in *The London Hermit, or Rambles in Dorsetshire,* a three act comedy performed in the Theatre Royal, Haymarket.

● The cross commemorates the village's twenty-two dead from the Great War and two who were killed in the Second World War.

● Turn left, up the narrow street, which is known as (and is) the Main Road. In a hundred yards, opposite the thatched range of Spindrift, No. 11 and the Old Bakery, you pass "The site of the Old Parish Church, pre-Norman in foundation. Demolished in 1860 when the present church was built."

● Just inside the gate is the grave of Obadiah Legg who died in 1912. To his left is a cross beneath the yew tree to several war heroes, including Charles William Haime, killed at Salonika, and Arthur Edward

Silverton, RN, commander of HMS *Defence*, who was lost in the Battle of Jutland. To the right is a stone to Robert Dudgeon, aged 29, who was the cook on board the *Avalanche*, from London, "drowned through her foundering after being in collision with the ship *Forest* in the English Channel, September 1877".

● In 150 yards, at the next junction — beside the Castle Inn — turn right into School Lane. After The Copse you come to Pond Plot bungalow.

● Between the bungalow and Beech Close you turn right, up the flight of steps between a paddock and the garden of thatched No.50.

● Turn left at the top, to "Youth Hostel, Range Walks". On reaching the field above the school you cross a stile and then turn right, uphill to a stile beside the army boundary fence.

● Cross this stile and continue uphill, signed "Range Walks when open", and keep the military lands to your left. Near the summit you come to the ditch and bank of an Iron Age entrenchment, which runs the length of Bindon Hill and protected a large Celtic settlement as well as their port which was Lulworth Cove.

● Turn right, following the "Bindon Hill" sign and walk beside the outer earthwork for 500 yards. At first you have a view to your right of West Lulworth, where you have just been walking. Ignore the ancient cross dyke which cuts up into the hill to your left as an additional line of defence.

● Instead you continue to the corner of the hillside, where Portland comes into distant view. The earthwork now bends to the left and you follow it around the corner of the hillside. Keep the car park to your right and head seawards as the Cove comes into view.

● Continue until you reach the cliff fence. Here you cross a stile and then turn right, descending with care the steep path that leads down to the beach, and boathouse of Lulworth Marine.

● Have an ice cream!

Arish Mell
& Fossil Forest

This is a strictly weekend, Saturday or Sunday, walk — for it explores the network of footpaths provided by the army across the western sector of the Lulworth tank gunnery ranges. Generally, these are open each weekend, and there are plenty of signs in the area that announce the position on the day.

However, if you want to make sure in advance, telephone the range office on 01929 462721. The army's "Provisional Firing Programme" is also published weekly in local newspapers. During August, and at the extended holidays of Christmas and Spring bank holidays, the walks are open during weekdays as well.

The walk, covering five miles, takes in the spectacular coast scenery at Mupe Bay, and also visits the famous Fossil Forest. The latter has an informative notice-board on site: "Many of the rocks of Purbeck began as sediments accumulating 120 million years ago in swamps. As the soil gradually builds up, large pine-like and fern-like trees grew here. Some of these stumps became fossilised, but only the former positions of the stumps, covered by a lime-type deposit, can now be seen. The Fossil Forest is part of a site of special scientific interest. It is an important part of our heritage and deserves your care, consideration and protection."

In other words, the stumps are only the shapes of the trees — not fossilised wood. Geological vandals who attack them with hammers to remove souvenirs take away bits of rock that are no different from the rest of the cliff.

Another point that needs emphasising is that our route has been chosen (at both the beginning and end) to avoid those sections of cliff which suffered landslips in early 1977, and it does not involve you walking any stretches of path which have been closed. Not that this guarantees dryness. Though the army paths are dry and firm, some of the edges of the range tend to become muddy, and boots should be worn. The cliff slopes are moderate to steep.

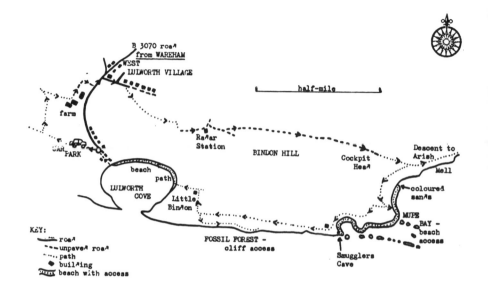

Park and start in the main car park at Lulworth Cove. The entrance is beside the turning circle at the end of the B3070, (Ordnance Survey map reference SY 822 801).

Leave the car park by the inland path-exit, marked by a stile and gate beside one of the "camping prohibited" signs. Walk along the wide gravel path across this field and go through the gate at the other end.

Immediately you are on the other side, turn right. You walk away from the well-marked paths and follow the fence, keeping it directly to your right. This track, between the hillside and a bramble thicket, runs up the valley towards West Lulworth village. At the end of the field the fence bends to the left and you come to a stile.

Cross the stile and then turn abruptly right, following the cattle track downhill into the farmyard. After the barns you turn left, passing Hambury House and sheds.

On reaching the tarred road you turn left for about 50 yards. Then turn right, up a lane marked Sunnyside, beside Cove House.

16

Thirty paces after this road becomes a track called Bindon Road, there is a gate and stile to your right.

● Cross this and walk uphill, keeping leftward, so that you climb towards the highest piece of the slope. Towards the summit you come to a grassy bank, and turn left to walk along it. This earthwork follows the side of the hill and marks the site of a timber palisade erected about 500 BC by some of the first Iron Age immigrants to cross the Channel from France. They used this bank to enclose a square mile of Bindon Hill, giving them undisputed use of both the sheltered anchorage at Lulworth Cove and the east-facing bay at Mupe. You also pass a cross-dyke, running over the top of the hill and giving protection to the colonists' eastern settlements. As you climb there is a sweeping view to the left, over Lulworth Camp, to Hamworthy.

● On reaching the boundary fence of the army lands you turn right and walk up to the mast. Here the notice on the gate should say "Lulworth Range Walks OPEN" if it is a day on which you can continue. Once inside the ranges you are asked to keep between the yellow banded posts — as the army only keeps the paths clear of explosives, and not the rest of the land.

● After you have passed the radar compound, continue straight ahead along the chalky track facing you. Fork left along the track signposted "Bindon Hill Walk." You keep on this path for a mile, to the clifftop at Cockpit Head, overlooking Mupe Bay. Just as you reach Cockpit Head there is a signpost pointing downhill to the "Coast Path" but you continue straight ahead at this point, aiming towards Worbarrow Tout and the Purbeck bays. Below the next stretch of path there is a steppes-like flatland with the green-brown hulks of more than a dozen tanks, with a whole history of their tracks visible across the plain for nearly a mile.

● At Arish Mell you can look, but do not touch. There is no path on to the beach. However, it is worth the effort — if only to look down from the cliff above — for the sea has broken through the chalk escarpment and is slowly eating a new bay into the flatter ground beyond. Lulworth Castle is visible in the trees at the head of the valley.

Turn round and walk back up the slope to the "Coast Path" signpost on Cockpit Head. Turn left, and walk down the steep slope. The actual path at this point starts descending the hill a short distance before you reach the signpost, and it is advisable to take it — you can then see where you are walking, and avoid having to stumble through long grass on the side of the precipice.

At the bottom, just after the "Coast Path" signposts, there is a flight of steps down on to the beach at Mupe Bay. This diversion is completely worthwhile as the army allows unrestricted access to Mupe beach. Its cliffs are multi-coloured sands, with a row of triangular rocks offshore. To the right, beyond the first line of Mupe Rocks, you come into a second cove. At the far end lies the Smugglers Cave. It is remarkable as it has a false-wall, about eight feet high, built across its back end. This wall encloses a chamber about 15 feet wide by ten feet deep. There are the remains of a door, though this could have been concealed by rocks. The main cave is forty feet deep.

On walking back to the top, to the signposts, take the left-hand of the two pointers. This path takes you along the clifftop for half a mile to Fossil Forest. As you pass above the Smugglers Cave you will notice the ruins of a small stone building, about eight feet square, which had its doorway facing the cliff edge and the open sea. A little further on is an interesting wartime pillbox with crinkle-cut walls, resulting from its concrete being poured into corrugated shuttering.

The path down to Fossil Forest is marked by a signpost: "Please do not damage the remains of fossil trees." The best three trunks are at the extreme eastern end of the ledges, which involves a little minor rock clambering about half-way along. They are hollow at the core and about six feet across. No longer vertical, they tilt with the strata at about 45 degrees towards the mainland. One pair were only growing about ten feet apart.

After walking back from the Fossil Forest you head inland to the lower of the red flags, and then turn left to leave the army ranges. The chapel cottage, Little Bindon, marks the site of a medieval monastery that finally closed down and moved itself to Wool. Resist the temptation to be too inquisitive. On the day we researched the walk a father and his herd of four children had penetrated to the bottom of the cottage garden. This sort of behaviour will provoke people into surrounding their photogenic homes with security fencing.

● Walk from the cottage down to the beach at Lulworth Cove, taking care over the last sticky hundred yards, and turn right along the beach. Walk to the Cove café and boathuts. From here a road leads to the car park. One enterprising youngster sometimes sells iron-pyrites as "local fools gold" from a tray on his garden wall.

Flower's Barrow
& Worbarrow

Entrenchments of a great prehistoric hill-fort cap the cliffs at the heart of the Lulworth Ranges. The earthworks dominate the western extremity of the Purbeck Hills where Flower's Barrow takes full advantage of the precipitous 565-feet high chalk cliff above Worbarrow Bay.

No defences were necessary along this southern side. This is the only Iron Age fortification in Purbeck and it appears to be of late date, about 50 BC.

It now encloses only four acres but at least half as much again must have fallen over the cliff. There are strong double banks on the landward approaches with the spaces between the ramparts being stretched at the west and east ends to keep the advantage of height over distance constantly with the defenders. The inner rampart at the east side stands six feet higher than the outer bank. These were key requirements for their slingstone weaponry. Pebbles used as slingstones were found in a 1939 excavation.

Depressions mark the sites of huts and underground grain stores. It is likely that Flower's Barrow was stormed by the Romans in AD 43-44, though a much fuller excavation would be necessary to prove that. A decapitated skeleton of "great stature" was found in the nineteenth century on the inner rampart.

Given the steep slopes, the sensible person's route to Flower's Barrow is to let the car do the hill climb and approach it from the car-park on the top of the Purbeck Hills at Povington Hill. Here you have a superb view over Tyneham valley to the south and across the immensity of the Army's Heath Range to the north.

This four mile walk, usable only when the Lulworth Range Walks are open — generally at weekends, public holidays and the month of August — then descends to what is left of the once picturesque stone-roofed fishing hamlet of Worbarrow. Cottages clustered around the deeply cut Gwyle stream, in the shadow of conical Worbarrow Tout and a setting that is still breathtakingly picturesque.

Westward rises the end of the Purbeck Hills, of white chalk cliffs at Flower's Barrow, from a foreground of myriad colours where Wealden sands spread through the spectrum with white, yellow, red, brown and purple hues.

Jack Miller's Sea Cottage, evacuated along with every home in Tyneham parish on 19 December 1943, is now just foundations. Likewise Worbarrow Coastguard Station, which has in the past been wrongly identified as the stone-built house closest to Pondfield Cove at the southern extremity of the hamlet, beneath Gold Down. I have been corrected by V. Watkinson who lived at Worbarrow until the autumn of 1943: "I notice that you still labour under the misapprehension that Hill Cottage was also the Coastguard Cottage. I'm afraid this is not so. My gran was born there, circa 1868. I was told that her father was born there, circa 1835, and I believe that his father was also born there.

"As you can see, this takes you back to the start of the nineteenth century!

"The Coastguard Station stood between Hill Cottage and the sea. The Coastguard at Worbarrow were disbanded somewhere around 1910-12. The old squire had the buildings demolished as soon as they left. You can, however, still see some trace of them if you look."

Another correspondent told me of "the great tragedy" that struck the men of Worbarrow Coastguard Station on a Saturday afternoon in March 1865. Five of them set sail to return from Weymouth in a galley laden with stores. They passed a gale warning, displayed from Admiral Fitzroy's signal opposite Weymouth Telegraph Station, forecasting southerly winds. These caught them about three miles from their base, when they were a mile off Lulworth Cove, and a watchman saw the sea strike the galley and sink her "like a stone". There were no survivors.

Inland, the route returns you to the Purbeck Hills via the evocative remains of the ghost village of Tyneham. Here the remains have survived somewhat better. In the case of St Mary's Church and the school the buildings are still intact and now function as museums.

They are shrines in a theme park where the Ministry of Defence manages an unlikely fusion of public access and tank gunnery.

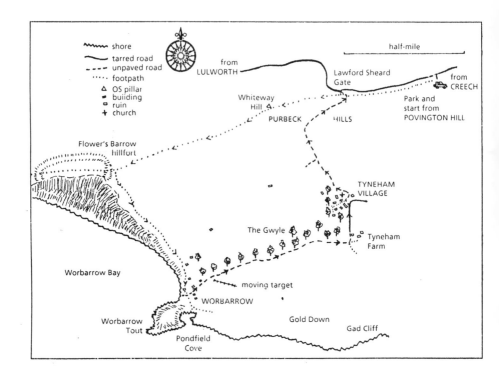

Legend:
- shore
- tarred road
- unpaved road
- footpath
- OS pillar
- building
- ruin
- church

from LULWORTH

Lawford Sheard Gate

half-mile

from CREECH

Whiteway Hill

Park and start from POVINGTON HILL

PURBECK HILLS

Flower's Barrow hillfort

TYNEHAM VILLAGE

The Gwyle

Tyneham Farm

Worbarrow Bay

moving target

WORBARROW

Worbarrow Tout

Gold Down

Gad Cliff

Pondfield Cove

● Park on top of the Purbeck Hills, midway between East Lulworth and Creech, in the Povington Hill car-park and picnic area (Ordnance Survey map reference SY 888 811).

● Head westwards, towards Portland, and leave the car-park through the gate beside red flag no.57, which is just north of firing point "D". Access is only possible when the gate is open, which will be the case if the Range Walks are in use.

● The grassy track runs along the spine of the Purbeck Hills, with Tyneham village to your left and the road to the right, for a third of a mile.

● In the dip you come to a stony track which rises out of the valley. Turn right and then immediately left to cross this. The track joins the public road at Lawford Sheard Gate but you keep on the military side of the barbed wire.

● Continue straight ahead, resuming the walk along the top

of the Purbeck Hills. The distant view is still Portland, with Lulworth Castle emerging from the inland woods to the right. Parallel lines of ancient banks are traceable in places, down the right-hand slope for 500 feet or more, below the Ordnance Survey triangulation pillar on Whiteway Hill. These were the Celtic field systems used by the occupants of Flower's Barrow hill-fort.

● The dirt track along the hilltop, used by armoured cars and Landrovers, extends for a mile and passes firing points "C", "B", and "A", plus a number of wooden target bearing points. Keep beside and between the army's yellow marker posts which delineate the safe path across this otherwise open landscape.

● The best clumps of orchids and other chalkland flowers are generally to the right of the path, which is marginally damper than the sun-scorched southern side.

● At Flower's Barrow you continue straight ahead, through the multiple banks and ditches of the fortifications, towards the other side, to soak in the stupendous views. This is some of the most spectacular coastal scenery in Europe, embracing Worbarrow Bay with Arish Mell beneath and the sweep of pebbles round to the line of offshore Mupe Rocks. Straight ahead, towards Bindon Hill, is Halcombe Vale, where Prime Minister Winston Churchill reviewed massed ranks of the new tank that bore his name — the Churchill — on 6 April 1942.

● When you have seen enough, turn back. This time, on leaving the earthworks, you turn right. Pass a seat and a 1940 anti-invasion pillbox. It has a superb view of the eastern half of Worbarrow Bay, and the coast onwards to St Alban's Head.

● Head towards Worbarrow Tout, which is the conical sugar-loaf projection of gypsum and Purbeck marble that juts into the bay, appearing like an island.

● Hereon it is difficult to descend with dignity. The long grass which is the speciality vegetation of the Lulworth Ranges can be as slippery as ice on this south-facing escarpment. Prepare to slide on your bum if you feel you are no longer going to be *Homo-erectus*. If you think this is bad, consider those struggling to climb up!

● In half a mile, after the pond, you pass the stone-walled

footings of Sheepleaze — the home of Tyneham Action Group chairman Philip Draper — and glimpse other ruins in out-of-bounds scrubland.

● Next is sea level, where you cross the Gwyle stream which may or may not flood across the pebbles depending on recent rainfall. The outline of Jack Miller's Sea Cottage is on the other side. Explore the beach and slipway. You are also allowed to climb the Tout and to venture into the delightful Pondfield Cove which is sheltered from westerly winds. It is also edged with military history, in the form of a double row of dragon's teeth anti-tank defences from the German invasion threat of summer 1940.

● Having seen Worbarrow's beach areas you turn inland from the slipway, up the dirt road that passes other remains of the little community. Bunker 28 is beside the railway track of a 300-metre moving target, stretching south-eastwards into the slope of Gold Down. It, of course, is off-limits.

● The old road follows the fence of the dense garlic-smothered woodland that engulfs the Gwyle. In half a mile the track bends to the left, just before the toilets, and bridges the little stream. The ruin is of a cart-shed which was one of the outbuildings of Walter Case Smith's Tyneham Farm. "Leatherjacket" was his nickname. "A cantankerous old sod," a nephew told me.

● Continue straight ahead through Tyneham car-park and walk down to the pond and Post Office Row, with its concrete K1 Mark 236 telephone kiosk of 1929.

● You then come to the water-spout inscription and oak tree that was planted by Margaret Bond for George V's coronation, in 1911.

● More diversions — you can visit St Mary's church, plus the wildlife display in the school, and the ruins of most of the cluster of buildings that comprise the village.

● Our path skirts the right-hand side of the churchyard and follows the old road northwards for half a mile to the Purbeck Hills.

● Here you climb Whiteway Hill diagonally, up a steep flinty incline. Continue straight ahead at the top, leaving Lawford Sheard Gate to the left, along the grassy path that is the last stage of the ascent to the hilltop car-park.

Tyneham:
Dorset's Ghost Village

I'll borrow the idea for this walk from the title of my book *Tyneham: Dorset's Ghost Village*. It is the special South Coast time-warp which went into military occupation six days before Christmas in 1943 under the orders of Winston Churchill's War Cabinet.

The takeover was for the training of the American and British tank crews who were to open the Second Front against the Nazis in Normandy. The whole parish of Tyneham and adjoining heathland and farmsteads were depopulated in order to expand the firing ranges for the Gunnery Wing of the Royal Armoured Corps Fighting Vehicles School at Lulworth Camp.

Co-beneficiaries of the Army's good fortune in being allowed to retain its war gains have been the animals and the birds. Military ecology, paradoxically, can win the green vote. It is superior to the county's normal countryside, the land that has since gone through the agricultural revolution of ploughing and chemicals, both in the numbers and diversity of its wildlife species.

That is why there are always buzzards circling overhead and why the peregrine falcon came back from near man-inflicted extinction to breed in the Lulworth Ranges ahead of its reappearance in civilian countryside. Other deft swing-wing birds of prey such as the merlin and hobby never stopped breeding in army lands when their like ceased to be seen in most of lowland England.

Tyneham and the ruins of its scattered farms and cottages have fared less well architecturally. In fact, during the abortive campaign for its release at the end of the 1960s, I published evocative postcards of six of its best buildings. With the exception of the church, all have since been reduced to their foundations, or only a single storey at most, in the name of conservation and safety.

Their remains are engulfed in a jungle that is still largely a forbidden land despite the network of permissive weekend and summer holiday paths, called the Lulworth Range Walks, that are opened when tank firing is suspended.

Most of the parish remains far from these paths. The system is concentrated along the coast and does particularly well in bringing public access to the former fishing hamlet of Worbarrow and its conspicuous Tout, plus the mile of tilting crags eastwards to the next summit of Tyneham Cap.

The views are spectacular and complement the breathtaking precipice which falls away only yards from your feet. Everywhere the colours change, from purple sands at Worbarrow to white chalk at Arish Mell, then grey shale at Kimmeridge, and yellow for the recent rock-falls of Purbeck stone. Portland and St. Alban's Head are the distant half-tones.

This five mile walk offers innumerable diversions. For a start, beside the car park at Tyneham, there is the village which can also be explored. En route, there are optional extras at Worbarrow. As well as the obvious great bay there is a delightful little cove at Pondfield, tucked away behind off-putting dragon's teeth anti-tank defences from 1940 when the potential invaders were the Germans. You can also climb the Tout.

Another diversion is to be mesmerised by the "nodding donkey" of the cliff-edge oilwell at Kimmeridge Bay. That is just the other side of the range boundary; the walk does a figure-of-eight circuit that keeps inside army lands.

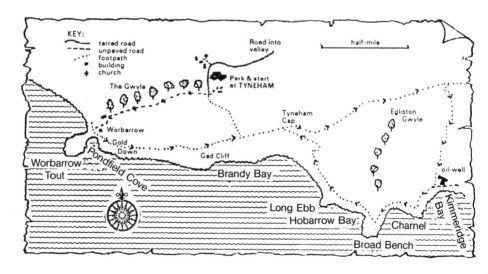

TYNEHAM: DORSET'S GHOST VILLAGE, page 2

● The Lulworth Range Walks are only open when the army is not firing. Signs between Lulworth and Wareham will show whether they are open or closed; generally they are open most Saturdays and Sundays, bank holiday Mondays, and for extended block leave periods during August and at Christmas through the New Year.

● The second proviso is that you keep to the paths, which tend to be about the width of a Landrover and run between yellow-painted marker posts.

● This walk starts from Tyneham village which lies in the coastal valley between East Lulworth and Kimmeridge, five miles south-west of Wareham. You turn south off the road across the top of the western Purbeck Hills, through a military gate (it will only be open if the walks are also available for use).

● Park in the car-park at Tyneham village (Ordnance Survey map reference SY 882 802). Put your back to the church and walk through the gate into the narrow sycamore wood in the floor of the valley.

● In 50 yards, on the other side of the trees, you turn right. This is the main track and is signed:

"Worbarrow Bay and Coastal Path". The gravel track follows the Gwyle, a Cornish word for uncultivated ground introduced here by the Williams family from Probus when they bought Tyneham House in 1567.

● In half a mile you will come to the ruins of the fishing hamlet of Worbarrow. The scenery is suddenly dramatic, being overlooked by Flower's Barrow hill-fort which lies end-on where the Purbeck Hills reach the sea. Arish Mell Gap, 550 feet below at sea level, is to the left. Next is Cockpit Head and Bindon Hill with Mupe Rocks sticking out into the Channel.

● At the beach, beyond the foundations of Sea Cottage, you look across to the bright colours of the Wealden sands, from red and purple through to yellow and white. Straight ahead is Worbarrow Tout, the conical-shaped projection that separates Worbarrow Bay from Pondfield Cove.

● Turn left, cross the stile and walk up the steep slope of Gold Down. Next are the mile-long crags of Gad Cliff, angled up into the sky with a precipice to your right. The coastal view opens out over Kimmeridge Ledges and Bay to St. Alban's Head on the horizon.

● Keep following the cliff path as you pass above Tyneham village. You now have another conical objective which is the summit of Tyneham Cap in another half mile. On its foothills the path turns right across a stile. You then fork left in 20 yards, along the upper option which is signed to "Kimmeridge Village".

● The 520-feet summit of Tyneham Cap has lost something of its romance and remoteness having been scalped and terraced by the army for a Landrover track. The stony road runs along the top of the ridge to the end of the ranges in half a mile. You pass above Egliston Gwyle, with its ruined farm, and then a set of medieval field strips which are visible on the upper slope immediately beneath the ridge. Stumpy brickwork and concrete beside the path, after the stile, mark the site of a wartime RAF coastal radar station.

● After the next stile you drop down to the army flag-pole and approach a gate at the range boundary. Do not go through it, but instead turn sharply right along a path that bends down the stony hillside between yellow markers. You are pointed seawards, towards "Kimmeridge Gate".

● On reaching the gentler slope you walk over to the fence, which is the range boundary. Keep it immediately to your left and walk to the cliffs, in half a mile, beside British Petroleum's "nodding donkey" or pump-jack oilwell. It has been pumping since 1959, from the Cornbrash limestone at 1,790 feet, and cumulative production is now in the region of half a millon tons.

● Turn right at the well-head, staying within the ranges, and follow the cliff path. The sea is to your left. The folly on the other side of Kimmeridge Bay is the Clavell Tower which was built by Rev. John Richards in 1831. On this side of the water there is an unusual circular pillbox from 1940.

● As the cliff path ascends your view is of the Lulworth Grounds fishing area and Portland on the far horizon. Brandy Bay, a delightful reminder of smuggling days, lies immediately to your left as the climb stiffens in the vicinity of Tyneham Cap.

● Here you leave the cliff and turn right and then left to skirt the steeper part of the escarpment. On the other side of Tyneham Cap the path levels off and you fork left, to a stile on the skyline.

● Continue straight ahead, again along the top of Gad Cliff, though this time with the sea to your left.

● In a quarter of a mile, just before the uppermost section of the cliff, there is a stone marker.

● Turn right here, downhill to "Tyneham". You drop towards Tyneham Farm and then diagonally cross the pasture to the left of it, across to a stile beside the main valley track. From here you continue straight ahead to the car-park, or take a diversion to the toilets to your right.

Kimmeridge
& Clavell's Hard

Kimmeridge is a neat stone and thatched village of just two streets that meet beside an ancient stone-roofed church at the foot of a limestone escarpment. A mile away, southwards, is the semi-circular shoreline of low, grey, oily cliffs that are the backdrop to Kimmeridge Bay.

It has a grandeur and a rough-edged beauty less certain than that of the stone cliffs of the Isle of Purbeck which resume on either side of the notorious Kimmeridge Ledges. These have claimed as many shipwrecks as the infamous Dead Man's Bay of the Chesil Beach at Portland.

The friable grey rock at Kimmeridge is perfumed with sulphur and has brought industry to this seaside for more than 2,000 years. Armlets were manufactured in the Iron Age as lathe-turned rings of imitation jet. The Romans achieved the miracle of pseudo-metallic furniture, again from this unlikely substance, which shone black for as long as it was kept oiled and polished.

Then it cracked and crumbled to bits. Meanwhile the locals braved or ignored the fumes and used lumps of shale as coal.

Industry beside the bay was revived in the 1560s with the extraction of alum for medicines and paints. Sir William Clavell not only expanded the enterprise in the seventeenth century but built a stone pier, which would be washed away in 1745.

By then his other venture, glass-making, had also failed. It was sited in a complex of furnaces, using the combustable shale to produce the heat for blowing the glass, across a site just north of the present fishermen's huts on the south side of the bay.

The next pier was constructed in 1848 by Wanostrocht and Company who also laid out a narrow gauge railway to bring the shale to a pier. It has since been reduced to two rows of rounded, pebbly stones that stretch across the wide beach. Gas was extracted from the rock, at a plant beside Weymouth backwater, and the company lit Wareham, in an experiment that won them the contract to take on the streets of Paris in 1858.

Efficiency, at 11,300 cubic feet per ton, was little less than that achieved from coal. Benzine was also extracted and then, in 1876, sanitary carbon was refined for sewer filters.

Some 5,000 feet of underground shafts were tunnelled inland from the cliffs south-east of the bay, at Clavell's Hard — a former landing beach, unusable now — and Rope Lake Head. The mining district was served by a new mineral railway, laid in 1883, which curved up the valley. Other initiatives followed until King Coal won the war and total closure took place in the 1890s.

Twentieth century explorations started with failures in the 1930s but then hit black gold at Kimmeridge Bay in 1959. The donkey-pump in the British Petroleum compound beside the Lulworth Ranges draws oil from 1,800 feet below, in the Cornbrash bed, and was the most productive on-land wellhead in the British Isles until the Wytch Farm discoveries, on the other side of Corfe Castle, in the 1970s.

This five mile walk approaches the former Coastguard Cottages at Gaulter Gap, which were built in the late 1820s. Several of their Customs and Excise occupants lie in Kimmeridge churchyard, beneath a row of gravestones that record drownings, "accidentally falling over the cliff" and "killed by his own firearms".

They used, as a lookout, the collonaded Clavell Tower, which was built as a clifftop folly by Rev John Richards in 1831. Richards assumed the name Clavell when he inherited the Smedmore estate in 1817.

Smedmore House was the seat of the Clavells. Their famous black sheep was gentleman robber John Clavell whose days as a highwayman nearly ended on the gallows in 1627. Instead he wrote a timely volume of poems entitled *A Recantation of an ill-led Life; or a Discoverie of the Highway Law*. They won him a pardon, from King Charles I, and were published by royal command.

Wrecking and smuggling were other local industries. Their recorded history spans seven centuries, from plundering of the stricken ship *Welfare* in 1371 to the tune of £2,000 which was a colossal amount in the values of the time — through to Kimmeridge's incorrigible smuggling Coopers. They were in and out of Dorchester Gaol in the early nineteenth century and when it came time to hang up the family grappling hooks and a half-anker spirit cask, these found their way on to the wall of the Dorset County Museum.

Another relic of industrial archaeology, the quarry at the top of Kimmeridge Hill — where Roman stone cists and other ancient remains have been found — provides a convenient starting point for the walk, at the point where roads come up the valley from Church Knowle and Steeple.

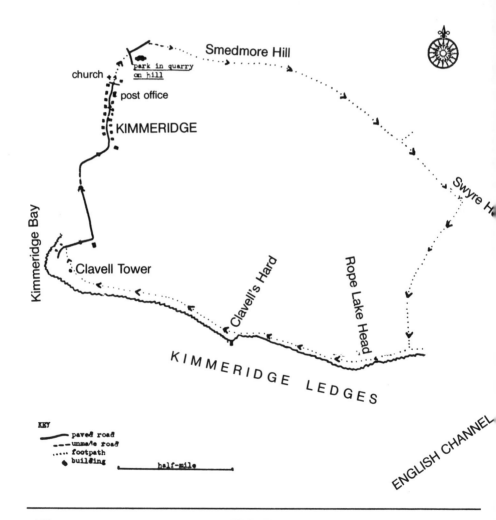

• Park and start in the quarry at the top of Kimmeridge Hill (Ordnance Survey map reference SY 918 800). This is six miles south of Wareham and three miles south-west from Corfe Castle. The quarry lies about 30 yards coastwards from the junction at the top of the hill, above Kimmeridge Bay. The quarry has a gravel surface, with space for twenty cars.

• Walk back to the junction, and turn right towards Church Knowle and Corfe Castle. Walk up the tarred road for about 80 paces and then turn right along a stony track. This goes through an iron gate and climbs uphill. The track runs for over a mile, beside a stone wall at the edge of the ridge, to the prehistoric burial mound at the top of Swyre Head. Here, at 666 feet, you have one of the finest views in Purbeck. It overlooks Encombe House and valley (spot the obelisk on the ridge to the left of the house) and you see Houns-tout and St Alban's Head in profile.

• As you reach the fence and stile beside the burial mound, you turn sharply right. In the corner of the field there is another stile, with a milestone pointing the way downhill to the "Coast Path". This is a permissive path: "The path beyond this point is not a public right of way but the owner allows the public to use it for the time being."

• You go downhill, keeping more or less in a straight line towards the sea. There is a stile at the end of the field, and another signpost after the length of dirt track.

• At the cliff you turn right. After about a hundred yards the blackstone ledges of grey bituminous shale begin to jut out into the water. The air has that Kimmeridge smell, and it is a mile and a half to the bay.

• In half a mile, at Clavell's Hard, you come to the second of three footbridges across small streams. This one, when it is flowing, leads to a waterfall with a drop of about 30 feet. On the other side of the water, until recent times, was an expanse of red and yellow rock stretching some 100 feet across the top of the outcrop — showing where the cliff caught fire and burnt for several months in 1973. Take a grey bit home to try on your fire! Commercial shale extraction was from a series of tunnels, now unsafe and inaccessible, that extend beneath the path and far inland.

• Continuing the walk, towards Kimmeridge, you see the bay's two landmarks. The Clavell Tower folly dates from 1831, and the oil field, from 1959. When the oil has finally gone, memories of scenes like this will bring waves of nostalgia.

• From the folly the path drops down to the bay. If you turn left, towards the coastguard hut, there is an excellent information board, its research by Dr D. P. Brachi. It explains the complex industrial archaeology of the shoreline, much of which has now been excavated.

• After you have seen the remains of the stone quays, follow the tarred road, which winds inland to the village. Near the top of the street is the Post Office stores, which stays open at weekends throughout the year. As well as tea and coffee it offers hot pies and a range of light snacks. Places on the coast that stay open for the locals during the winter are deserving of your support.

• From the Post Office you continue to the top of the village street, and climb the church steps. You keep walking straight ahead, along the flagstone path beside the church wall.

• This path continues into the field and climbs to a gap in the hill on the skyline. Scattered stones near the top mark the remains of a wall and stone stiles.

• At the top, after an electricity pole, you cross a stile and turn right on to the tarred road. The quarry, and your car, are about forty paces further, on the left.

Encombe's
Golden Bowl

Encombe is Purbeck's perfect valley. It is the remarkable Golden Bowl, created by a swirl of hills from the inland summit of Swyre Head around to Houns-tout Cliff, protecting not only the house but also its lawns, lake and woods from all the drawbacks of a location a thousand yards from the sea.

The great house complements the superb situation. It has a pleasantly simple south-facing frontage that was completed in 1770, when it housed a branch of the influential Pitt family.

Seawards Encombe's South Gwyle ends with a waterfall into Egmont Bight, between Kimmeridge and Chapman's Pool. Here the great headland off Houns-tout-Cliff, flat-topped at 500-feet, overlooks the cove of Chapman's Pool, which despite its often benign appearance is not a safe anchorage. The cliffs are also unsafe, being grey shale clays capped by a band of yellowish Purbeck stone, liable to mud-flows and landslips.

This five mile walk makes a complete circuit of Encombe's Golden Bowl, and brings you the full length of the coastal plateau that terminates abruptly with a view from the limestone crags over St Alban's Head and Chapman's Pool. You look down on the stone-roofed boathouse that was built as a lifeboat station after 1866 when "the great loss of life and property on this part of the coast have at length aroused the attention of the government and we are happy to say that the preparations have commenced for placing a lifeboat in this little bay".

It had to close, however, as difficulty launching made its use impossible in severe weather. Immediately below the summit of Houns-tout is Egmont Point, from which Rev Malcolm Piercy and Frank Lander saved seven men thrown exhausted on to the rocks on 10 January 1920 when the new 5,200-ton freighter *Treveal* was abandoned a mile off shore.

Thirty-six of their colleagues drowned. The ship later broke in two but the sections floated for days, before sinking to eight fathoms. Her cargo of manganese from Calcutta — it was the last leg of the maiden voyage — is still largely intact.

The visible history is that of the Scott family who came in 1807 when William Morton Pitt sold Encombe to John Scott. He would be created first Earl of Eldon and was Lord High Chancellor of England just about continuously from 1801 through to 1827. Described as "almost the ideal of manly beauty", he was the last bastion of cabinet resistance against the reforms that others were reluctantly accepting as inevitable — including those extending voting rights, abolishing rotten boroughs such as Corfe Castle, and emancipating Roman Catholics.

Eldon was never happier "than when among the birds at Encombe" but, his brother William complained, he could "kill nothing but time".

Sir William Scott, the first Baron Stowell, was a close friend of Dr Johnson and the pre-eminent draughtsman of international maritime law. His monument is the 40-feet high obelisk, tapering in Egyptian needle-style and constructed in blocks of Seacombe stone, which stands above Quarry Wood at the head of Encombe Valley. Lady Frances Jane Bankes laid the foundation stone on 28 May 1835.

Lord Chancellor Eldon's landscape memorial is Eldon Seat, on the undercliff of Swyre Head. It is a superb block of Purbeck stone, eight feet long and four feet wide, with another massive ashlar as the backrest. They are set on a raised podium, with the first stone being laid by Lady Elizabeth Repton on 15 October 1835.

She had eloped with architect George Stanley Repton, the youngest son of landscape-gardener Humphry Repton. Young George designed the rebuilt church of St James at Kingston, in 1833, which has a stone plaque recording that its predecessor was "much decayed". It is now a house.

That new church became the "old" one between 1874 and 1880 with the creation of the present St James's church as the last great flourish of Purbeck marble, virtually on a cathedral scale. The final major achievement of architect George Edmund Street, a skilful medieval restorer as well as a gothic revivalist, it was, he said, his "jolliest" job. No expense was spared by the third Earl of Eldon in erecting what was, in effect, a colossal private chapel.

Church historian Fred Pitfield, writing in *Purbeck Parish Churches*, praises its authentic thirteenth century details and the lavish use of

Purbeck marble for the shafting of the arcade piers. It is, he says, the finest example of Purbeck stonework that you can find in the Isle of Purbeck itself.

Both churches are conspicuous landmarks on the edge of the limestone plateau, overlooking the central vale of Purbeck and looking across to Corfe Castle in the gap of the Purbeck Hills. The B3069 climbs into Kingston from this direction.

As for the walk itself, be prepared for one stiff climb, and listen for "Portland" on the shipping forecast if the wind is gaining strength. Don't go if there is a gale warning.

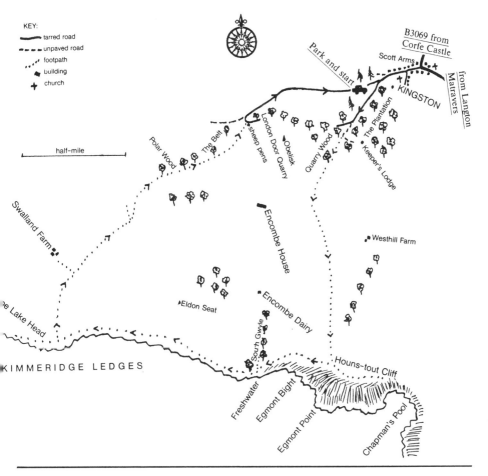

- Park in Kingston, up from the Scott Arms on the same side of the main street as the pump, or beside the cottages in South Street. Alternatively, if there is no space, continue up the main street to the level stretch in the woods, 50 yards after the "Encombe Dairy" sign. Park on the left, in the trees (Ordnance Survey map reference SY 953 794).
- Either way, given you are so close, start by visiting St James's church. Then continue up the main street. A hundred yards after the top end of the churchyard the road forks in three directions.
- Take the centre option, which despite the "Private No Entry" sign is also the "Footpath to Hounstout". This untarred road runs between The Plantation and Quarry Wood.
- In a third of a mile, at the next set of junctions, you again take the centre option, which is a stony track that forks left from the tarred drive down to Encombe House. You are to keep on the high ground. Enjoy the graffiti, if it is still there. For the record, if "Yeltsin is a CIA stooge" then Encombe knew it first.
- In a further hundred yards you pass the drive to the Nursery Tea Room and continue straight ahead along a grassy farm track. Encombe House and obelisk are to your right.
- To the left is an old stone wall which you follow to the cliffs, in a mile. There are stone seats en route, as indeed you'll find for the duration of this delightful walk. The view over the English Channel can be admired in comfort from that to Michael Byrne, 1923-80. Here our walk turns right, towards "Kimmeridge 3, Swyre Head 2¼".
- But first follow the coast path the other way, for the classic view from 500-feet above Chapman's Pool and St Alban's Head, which is one of the most beautiful on the whole South Coast.
- Having then turned westwards to resume the walk, towards Portland and Kimmeridge, you descend to Egmont Bight and the remains of Freshwater Steps, which are NOT to be followed as they lead to a death-drop beside a waterfall. This cascades on to an inaccessible beach.
- Seawards jut the first of the treacherous Kimmeridge Ledges. To your right, above the second field, you can glimpse Eldon Seat, dated 1835, and the gravestone to

the Lord Chancellor's "favourite dog Pincher, a German spaniel, who died May 19th 1840".

• Follow the cliff path for a mile, westwards from Freshwater Steps towards Rope Lake Head.

• Here you turn right and follow the low bank, at the edge of the field, which is the Kimmeridge parish boundary. This is a permissive path which climbs straight up Swyre Head, the great grassy inland promontory. You ascend to the prehistoric round barrow at 672-feet above sea level. The view on a clear day is from Portland Bill to St Catherine's Point, then left along the Isle of Wight to the Needles.

• Your path is now "Kingston 2", across the middle of the field on the other side of the fence from the burial mound. The triangulation pillar is to your left and below, to the right, is Encombe House.

• Follow the stone wall, which then runs beside the wind-clipped sycamores of Polar Wood. You are heading towards the obelisk and the Needles.

• At the end of the field you go through the kissing gate and now head left of centre, towards the tower of Kingston church. It is just visible above the trees.

• In the middle of the field the path bends to the left and descends to the sheep pens beside a wood that conceals the disused London Door Quarry.

• From the pens a tarred road leads up through stone gate posts.

• On the other side of these, turn immediately right. You are now walking gradually uphill, along the straight tarred section of the lane. In a mile you are back in Kingston, with the woodland car-park being concealed in the conifers to your right.

Worth Matravers
& St Alban's Head

St Alban's Head is a Dorset place-name that arouses passion. Usage of this local and maritime pronunciation will be denounced in letters from Dorset incomers and the county's away-band of devotees in cosy Home County suburbia. They are perfectly correct in their pedantry — that it is named for Capella Sancti Aldelmi, the exquisite Norman chapel on the headland.

St Aldhelm was the Saxon saint who was bishop of Sherborne from 705 to his death in 709. On the other hand, St Alban — the first British martyr — was from the Hertfordshire town that carries his name.

The problem is that I have never heard any native of Purbeck, or a Dorset countryman, refer to it other than as St Alban's Head. John Smeaton, who built the Eddystone lighthouse in the 1750s, called it that when he came to sample the stone, as did the first map-makers. All the navigation charts followed their example. This rocky promontory is the southern tip of the Isle of Purbeck. It is an isolated 350-feet cliff with underside quarry ledges and a precipitous stone pillar left as a sea-mark. Offshore is a turbulent tide-race.

On the top is a Norman chapel, Victorian coastguard cottages and an operational lookout, plus the footings of a Second World War radar station. Otherwise it is an utterly featureless setting amid flat fields. The plateau is known locally as The Plain. When you stand beside the chapel the view is nothing much other than sea. The headland juts out so much further than the rest of the Isle of Purbeck, into the English Channel, and you have to turn sideways to see any land. Much the most interesting approach is to plan your walk along the cliff path, such as in this five mile circuit, rather than using the boring mile-long route from Worth Matravers village via Renscombe Farm.

Coming to this coast in the July sun is to see a hostile landscape at its most deceptively benign. It is quite another matter to be in, or even above, these waters in a hurricane, or indeed any strong wind, either in winter or summer. The roll-call of wreck and rescue is as great as anywhere between the Lizard and the Goodwin Sands, with the single exception of Dead Man's Bay in the corner of the Chesil Beach at Portland. Of the multitude of calamities, either side of St Alban's Head, two have left physical reminders. The great tragedy was the *Halsewell*. An East Indiaman, outward bound from London for Bengal, she was dashed to pieces on the cliffs between Seacombe and Winspit in "a remarkable snow storm, sometimes a hurricane, with the wind at the south" at 02.00 hours on 6 January 1786. The Worth parish register records that the ship was shattered to pieces, and a very small part of her cargo saved. "It proved fatal to 168 persons, among whom were captain (Richard Pierce), two of his daughters, and five other young ladies." Eighty-two lives were saved.

In the sea in 1967 three Swanage divers found a cannon from the *Halsewell* and recovered coins, cannon balls, furniture hinges, lead shot, tackle and glass. Their prize find was the ship's pintle; the bronze hinge which held the rudder. The items are now in the Dorset County Museum at Dorchester. On land the wreck site is marked by the great slanting Halsewell Rock — on to which the eighty-two survivors climbed and clung — with the Halsewell Quarry and its quarrymen's cave drawings of the disaster being half way up the cliff, and the Halsewell Stile is in the old stone wall at the top.

The loss of the newly built *Treveal* was Purbeck's tragic shipwreck of the twentieth century. There were only seven survivors. Thirty-six drowned, and only twenty-one bodies were recovered. A stone cross in the north-east corner of Worth churchyard reads: "Here lie the unidentified bodies of two of the crew of the *SS Treveal* drowned on January 10th, 1920, when their ship was wrecked off St Alban's Head with the loss of 36 lives."

Standing on St Alban's Head is St Aldhelm's Chapel, a square all-stone buttressed Norman building of circa 1170, with walls ten metres square and a pyramidal roof supported by a massive central column. This has twelve chamfered corners and eight arches springing outwards to the centre of the walls and the four corners. It is sited at 379-feet altitude. It has been said that there was no cross until 1873 but one is shown on

Julia M Colson's drawing of the 1850s. However, the column originally supported something heavier, such as a bell cupola. There are no stairs to indicate that it was surmounted by a sea-warning beacon, which was an attractive Victorian theory.

The very cliffs are now monuments to human endeavour, being shelved and literally undermined with great chambers from which massive quantities of stone were extracted between 1690 and 1945.

These coastal beds are truly Portland stone and from the uppermost stratum of the Jurassic system. They are marine in origin, whereas the Purbeck beds that carry the area name are inferior freshwater limestone. Fossils show the difference.

What you don't see on the walk, apart from a single surviving building, is Britain's most important defence research establishment of the Second World War. The rest, and all masts and aerials, have been removed. This was the Telecommunications Research Establishment which was evacuated to Worth from Dundee in 1940 and played a key role in the secret war.

Radar was already being deployed, at St Alban's Head amongst other places, along the front-line coast, but TRE's crucial discovery was radio countermeasures that won the "Battle of the Beams" against Luftwaffe radio navigation. Otherwise there would have been a Coventry raid every night.

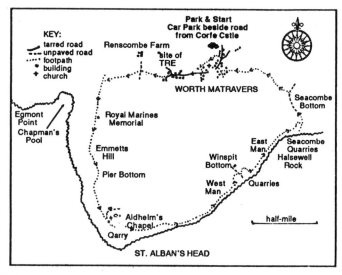

● Park and start from the village car-park in Worth Matravers, which is on the west side of the approach road from Corfe Castle (Ordnance Survey map reference SY 974 776). Walk down the road towards the Square and Compass for a hundred yards. Immediately opposite the north gable of the stone-roofed public house turn right, up a track signposted: "Footpath to Church and Hill Bottom ¾." In 50 yards turn left, over a stone stile, and follow the left-hand side of the field. Walk straight across the northern extension of St Nicholas's churchyard, leaving by the stile in the opposite hedge.

● In a hundred yards, in the next corner of the field, turn left across a stile and then go straight ahead. Use the dirt track immediately left of Bladon's tarred drive and cross the stone stile into a field. Keep the ivy covered stone wall to your right. Exit through the kissing gate and turn right along the tarred road. Walk to Weston Farm and silo, in 250 yards, and continue along the road to the corner which is beside the last of the farm buildings.

● Here, beside stone roofed Old Harry Cottage, you turn left. The path is signed: "Footpath to St Aldhelm's Head 1½." In only 80 yards, at the end of the first field, turn right. Leave the concrete farm road and cross a stile on to a dirt path signed: "Chapman's Pool 1." The next stile brings you into a field and you continue straight ahead, following the right-hand fence. The fields on the other side, across to Renscombe Farm and beyond both its roads, mark the site of the wartime Telecommunications Research Establishment. They used to be full of huts and masts.

● Go straight across the stony road to the stile on the other side. This path is signed: "Chapman's Pool ¼." Walk diagonally along this long field, heading left of centre, to the stile on the far side. It is beside the stone walled corner. Walk straight across the next field, to the clifftop stone wall. Cross the stile which overlooks Chapman's Pool and Houns-tout Cliff, with Egmont Point beneath, which was the scene of the 1920 *Treveal* drownings.

● Turn left along the cliff path. The stone wall is to your left and the English Channel some four hundred feet below to your right.

As the wall becomes a fence, on Emmett's Hill, you pass the stone table and benches built by the Dorset branch of the Royal Marines Association to the memory of all Royal Marines killed between 1945 and 1990: "Rest awhile and reflect that we who are living can enjoy the beauty of the sea and countryside."

● In half a mile you descend into Pier Bottom and climb up the other side, on to St Alban's Head. You pass the Norman chapel and coastguard lookout, and come next, in a mile, to the medieval strip lynchets on the side of East Man. These were cultivated terraces but are now under grass.

● You descend into the deep-cut quarried chine of Winspit. On dropping down to the valley track you turn right and then immediately left to cross it. Climb the steps above the iron-grilled bat roost which is home for the rare Greater Horseshoe species. Follow the cliff path. Ignore the first stile and continue straight ahead to the next in half a mile. This is set in an old stone wall immediately above the shore-line Halsewell Rock (don't even try to see it!) and here you enter National Trust land.

● The path skirts inland and brings you down into Seacombe Bottom. Turn right, to go down to the shelving ledges and see the breathtaking undercliff quarries from the correct side of the safety fence. Then head inland, up the valley, and follow the main path for a third of a mile. Towards the head of the valley you leave it and fork leftwards into a grassy coombe.

● At the end of this scrubby pasture you start to ascend. Go over the stile and climb another towards the top of the hill. Continue straight ahead between two fields and then cross another stone stile. You walk directly across this wide valley, down the slope and then up the other side. Leave the sheep down at a stile between two houses at the top of the opposite slope. A stony passageway leads to a track which brings you up to the picturesque duck and toad pond on the village green. Unusually, the village toad is the Natterjack which is particularly surprising as they normally burrow in sand.

● Turn right and then fork left, below the Square and Compass, to return to the car-park.

Dancing Ledge
& Seacombe

The National Trust's recent Dorset acquisition encompasses the finest piece of "civilian" scenery which the Trust did not already own in the Isle of Purbeck. The parenthesis is to exclude the incomparable military ranges. Almost up to their quality is the 1992 purchase of 183-acre Spyway Farm which includes most of the parish of Langton Matravers that lies between the village and the sea.

Its sheep-grazed limestone downland is rich in orchids and the sheer cliffs of Purbeck stone have the last puffin colony on the Dorset coast, now marking the extremity of their range eastwards up the English Channel.

Best of all, from a landscape point of view, is the man-made Dancing Ledge. It was literally cut from the cliff by Victorian quarrymen who composed a veritable three-dimensional seascape with an outer shelf that is fringed with kelp and lapped by the waves.

Above are two terraced working floors, with the remains of cliff-cut galleries behind, facing due south and sheltered from hostile winds.

The surrounding expanse of stone plateau turf is crossed by the ancient Priest's Way and slots in perfectly, on the side towards Worth Matravers, with the existing Trust-owned lands which were bequeathed by estate owner Ralph Bankes in 1981. These two areas are scenically one, with the landscape opening out westwards into the best limestone valley in the county, beneath Eastington, and a continuing series of quarries culminating in the greatest underground workings in Dorset, notched into the side of Seacombe Bottom.

These cliff-hanging galleries are twelve feet in height, having yielded two layers of fine stone, called the basebed and whitbed. The latter at Seacombe was eight feet thick, compared with seven feet in the sister quarry half a mile south-west at Winspit.

One of the special jobs accomplished with Seacombe's thick seam was the making of a 3½-ton trough for the North Woolwich Galvanising Works in 1871. The great stone, produced at A. Bower's quarry, was eight feet long, four feet wide and four feet deep.

To the west, at the extremity of the Trust's holding, is the slanting Halsewell Rock. The only one to extend above the splash-zone of the sea, it permitted the miracle rescue of those who escaped Purbeck's worst shipwreck, which drowned 168 crew and passengers of the *Halsewell* in a blizzard at two o'clock in the morning of 6 January 1786.

She was a 758-ton East Indiaman, outward bound for Bengal, captained by Richard Pierce who was accompanied by two daughters, two nieces and three other young ladies: "Some of the Officers and Seventy-one Seamen and Soldiers with great difficulty escaped upon the Rock. But Captn. Pierce, seeing it was impossible to preserve the lives of his daughters, refused to quit the Ship and therefore perished along with them."

Boats still come to grief along the stone wall of southern Purbeck and, on the afternoon Matthew Roche and I researched the route for this five-mile walk, we had a grandstand view of a Royal Navy Sea King helicopter from Portland, hovering off-shore as a crewman dangled from it. He was being lowered to help a yacht listing beside the strong tide-race that surges off St Alban's Head.

On land there are no difficulties with the route. It is almost wholly across National Trust land and entirely along well-marked and signed dry paths. Definitely the best walking country in Dorset!

● Park in Langton Matravers, which is on the B3069 two miles west of Swanage. The walk begins from the middle of the village street, at Durnford Drove (Ordnance Survey map reference SY 997 788). There is ample roadside parking in the village, particularly at the upper end, towards Corfe Castle, opposite the Top Shop.
● In Durnford Drove you pass the "1st Langton B.P. Scout and Guide H.Q. 1953" which also has a foundation stone in the wall beside the pavement: "Erected by voluntary service of the scout and guide packs and friends aided by the scouts. Opened by Ralph Reader, May 1954." He was the national Gang Show compère.
● At the end of the road, after Gyphayes and the last bungalow, Arbutus, you continue straight ahead through the gates. Walk up

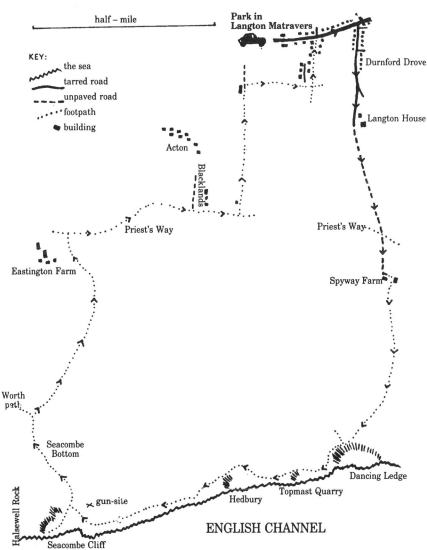

half – mile

KEY:
the sea
tarred road
unpaved road
footpath
building

Park in Langton Matravers

Durnford Drove

Langton House

Acton

Blacklands

Priest's Way

Priest's Way

Eastington Farm

Spyway Farm

Worth path

Seacombe Bottom

Halsewell Rock

gun-site

Seacombe Cliff

Hedbury

Topmast Quarry

Dancing Ledge

ENGLISH CHANNEL

the slope and follow the drive beside the walled grounds of Langton House. This becomes a stony track and crosses a field, to Spyway Farm which is on the skyline.

● You cross the Priest's Way and walk up to the barn, following the arrow to "Dancing Ledge ¾". After passing between the barn and the farmhouse you continue straight ahead, towards the sea.

● As you reach the ridge above the water you pass another stone pointer to Dancing Ledge. Head a little right of centre and descend the slope. Cross the left-hand stile at the bottom and drop down onto the quarry floor. On the lower level, where the waves dance across the ledge, there is a rough-hewn rectangular swimming pool which was cut by quarrymen so that the boys of Durnford School could have their daily nude dip irrespective of sea conditions.

● Return to the top and turn left, across the first stile. You are now heading westward along the "Coast Path, Seacombe 1". The next little cliffside working is Topmast Quarry. After it is the much larger Hedbury Quarry, with a George III cannon, six feet long, mounted as a display piece.

Seaward of it is a "whim-stone" which supported a derrick used for lowering blocks of stone into boats.

● There are another couple of smallish quarries but the following set of workings, in half a mile, stretch along the end of the valley at Seacombe Bottom. These high chambers are the largest and most extensive galleries in the Isle of Purbeck.

● To the right, on the brow of the hill overlooking the valley, is a discreetly sited 1940 anti-invasion pillbox of an exceedingly rare type. It is domed, with a cockpit-shaped revolving steel hood, five feet in diameter, with a tunnelled entrance and a slit for the machine-gunner.

● In the valley, you will see that the National Trust has fenced off the quarries, which are visibly unsafe with collapsing entrances. There is, however, a public path across the cliffside quarry floor, and this is still accessible and at a safe distance from the main workings.

● On reaching the sea, and glimpsing the slanting Halsewell Rock just to the right of the next set of quarry shelves which are towards Winspit, you turn round and head inland. Our walk leaves the coast path and heads along the stony track through Seacombe Bottom. Initially it is signed "Worth 1".

● In 500 yards, however, you ignore the "Worth" arrow and continue along the main track as it bends to the right. Just around the corner you cross a stile beside a gate.

● The next section of the valley is a superb expanse of limestone grassland, half crossed by just a single stone wall which has been neatly rebuilt by the National Trust.

● At the head of the valley, in half a mile, you cross a stile beside a gate and then come to a second gate, 150 yards from Eastington Farm.

● Turn right here, along Priest's Way. Follow this for half a mile, passing the active stone-pits around the quarrymen's hamlet of Acton. You are now heading east and Swanage Bay and the Purbeck Hills come into view.

● Pass the track that is signed to Acton and a notice stating "No Unauthorised Vehicle Beyond This Point".

● About 200 yards from here, after Blacklands chalet which has a line of cottages behind it, you turn left through a gateway. This path is on a terrace which is slightly higher than the field. Signed "Langton ¾", it runs beside a stone wall, to your left, and passes a stone-roofed barn.

● Continue straight ahead along the terraced path in the next field and pass under a power line. Then leave the field and walk beside the cottages.

● Ten yards after the end of the terrace, which is No. 1, you turn right through a kissing gate. Here you have two options. You can go left of centre, diagonally across the field, to emerge in Langton opposite the Top Shop. Alternatively, you go straight ahead, following the right-hand wall, to find the centre part of the village.

● This path then passes a garden and goes straight across a tarred road. Keep straight on, to the other side of a small paddock, and then cross the wall.

● Turn left and follow power cables into the village. You come into the main street just down from the 1875 Methodist church opposite Old Malthouse Lane, which is a short distance up from Durnford Drove.

49

Priest's Way
& Dancing Ledge

The quarrylands of Purbeck are best explored from the Priest's Way which takes its name from the early Middle Ages when Worth Matravers had the priest and Swanage was merely a fishing hamlet to which he tramped each week. Scenically, the best section is between Acton and Belle Vue, to the south of Langton Matravers village, and this five mile walk also takes in a precipitous length of the stone-cliffs westwards to the old quarries at Dancing Ledge where the loads were taken out by boat, and then re-exported via Swanage.

For most of the year it is a botanist's delight. That was literally so the day I researched the walk, for I noticed down the cliff a clump of pure white thrift with larger than normal flowers. Nearby I spotted a botanical expedition and led them to the spot, away from their lady's slipper orchids.

"Extraordinary!" one of them exclaimed, as 80-year-old flora author John Fisher, from Chichester, strode seawards and unhitched his cameras. Beside us stretched the nylon ropes of real climbers, who had very nearly had a close encounter with a tangle of 1940 anti-invasion wire.

I found it on the path and did my public duty. As I got it to the edge and was about to deliver the final seaward toss I saw a bright splash of colour which turned out to be one of their ropes with three harlequins directly below. The barbed wire was left for a gale to send it down.

The other excitement was knowing I was walking above the best bit of industrial archaeology in Dorset, namely the Purbeck stone mine-shaft at Belle Vue, but there is no access to that from the rights of way network.

All that disappointed me was the almost complete absence of seabirds at the height of the breeding season. It was nice to see fulmar, shag and jackdaw — but distressing that there was only one of each. I am not old enough to remember the cliffs actually teeming with auks but even in my time it used to be a futile exercise trying to count them. We are all diminished by their passing, which is all the sadder for the visual perfection of the seascape which belies the disaster that has taken place.

As for the walk, it starts from the B3069 which is the higher road between

Corfe Castle and Swanage, via Kingston and Langton Matravers. The paths are well marked, generally firm and dry, and almost entirely unobstructed. The only point where I strayed from the right of way a group of children were playing and one shouted: "You're off the path, mate!"

I approached him to ask where it went — since correctly sorted out for the text — but they fled. Sensible, I suppose, but it is a sad comment on the fear that underlies modern life.

● Park and start from the B3069 at the top end of Langton Matravers village. The street is wide enough for roadside parking above Toms Field Road, (Ordnance Survey map reference SY 994 788).

● Walk down the main street. On the left, opposite St George's school playing fields, stood Durnford School which was the birthplace in 1899 of Tudor biographer Hester Chapman, and housed pioneer radar boffins of the Telecommunications Research Establishment in 1940-42. It was demolished in about 1950.

● Turn right into Durnford Drove, passing the stone-built scout hut that was opened by gang-show compere Ralph Reader in May 1954. At the end of the housing estate the public path follows the tarred drive beside the wall of Langton House, continues through a gate and becomes a stony "Private Road" to Spyway Barn.

● Turn left at the end of this field, before you reach the buildings, at the point where the power cables cross the road. This track is the Priest's Way, heading towards Swanage. Follow it straight ahead, towards the bay and the Isle of Wight, for half a mile.

● Then continue straight ahead along a lesser trackway to the stone-roofed buildings at South Barn. Here the historic route continues straight ahead as an overgrown depression, from which the present right of way strikes off sharply to the left, passing the corner of South Barn and following its drive away from the house.

● Cross the cattle-grid and turn right along the track. Keep going straight ahead, across a stone stile, at the next corner. You cross a pasture as you approach the next set of buildings, Belle Vue Farm.

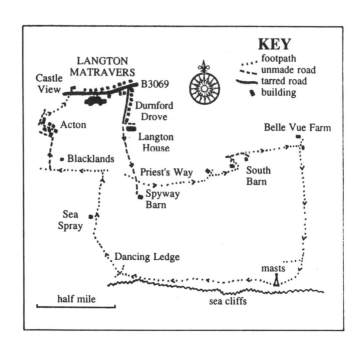

KEY

. . . . footpath
‒ ‒ ‒ unmade road
‒‒‒‒ tarred road
▮ building

LANGTON MATRAVERS

Castle View

B3069

Durnford Drove

Acton

Langton House

Belle Vue Farm

Blacklands

Priest's Way

South Barn

Spyway Barn

Sea Spray

Dancing Ledge

masts

half mile

sea cliffs

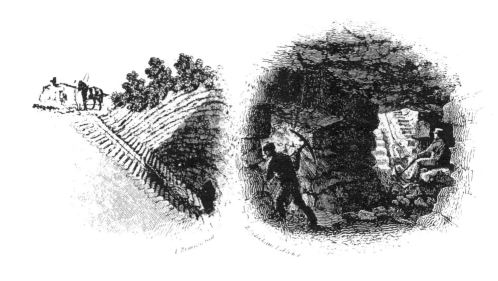

• Turn right beside a cluster of Victorian quarry sheds. These are the best preserved in the Isle of Purbeck, containing a perfect pair of capstan grab-stones, work benches, and a superb "slide" shafting down thirty feet to underground tunnels. All this history is definitely off-limits and your path is the one southwards, up and out of the Swanage valley and on to the limestone plateau above the English Channel. The last field is owned by the National Trust, as is the rest of the walk.

• Descend to the cliff path. Turn right, passing the masts which mark one end of a measured mile, for the purpose of speed tests in sea-trials. The current set was constructed by Balfour Beatty in 1986.

• In half a mile you drop down to sea level at the former cliff quarries of Dancing Ledge. The rectangular rock-pool in the lower shelf, towards the left end, was cut by the quarrymen for the boys of Durnford School; they had daily swims and it was a school rule that they bathed naked.

• On returning to the cliff path, walk straight ahead inland, taking the path just left of centre, into a dip in the hills signed "Langton 1¼".

You cross a stile, climb on to the ridge, and go through a gate on to a track. This stretches for a third of a mile, passing Sea Spray, the cottage across the fields, and a quarry.

• You come to the Priest's Way and turn left along it, towards the quarrying hamlet of Acton. In a third of a mile the main track bends to the right and leads you past Blacklands and into Acton.

• Take the track to the right of the first house and walk up to Quarry Cottage. Immediately to its left you cross a stone stile and walk down an alley.

• Then turn left, passing Lane End Cottage. Follow this narrow street to the tarred road. Here you turn right, passing a range of typically long and squat stone-roofed and gutterless traditional Purbeck cottages, and then the contrasting 1896 loftiness of Fernlea.

• Immediately after Fernlea you turn right, crossing the stile into a field, and head towards the left-hand end of Swanage Bay. From the clump of scrub you turn leftwards and leave the field at the gate facing Castle View Cottage.

• Turn right on to the road, which is the B3069, and walk down to your car.

Durlston
Country Park

Cliffs south of Swanage were selected in the early 1970s for Dorset's first country park and a significant holding of council land, already highly popular with visitors, was expanded by leasing adjoining fields. This was a Victorian and Edwardian playground and overflows with the history of seaside tourism as well as important wildlife habitats.

In 1974 Durlston Country Park was opened. County planning officer Alan Swindall explained that the management plan had been designed to preserve "the rich ecological pattern" by a "careful balance between people and nature". It includes some of the last sea-cliff nesting sites of the auks, and concentrations of orchids across Round Down. Inland the park extends for half a mile, to within one field of California Farm, Durlston Farm and South Barn. On the western edge it joins the National Trust's Belle Vue holding.

The long-running friction between naturalists and climbers has been smoothed by a compromise that creates sanctuaries and areas with a closed season, but allows unrestricted access elsewhere.

Some of the climbs rank amongst the most popular in the country and the classic ones have their own names, including Rendezvous Manque between Durlston Head and Tilly Whim Caves, and Traverse of the Gods between the caves and the lighthouse. At the side of the headland is the Subliminal Cliff. Westwards from Anvil Point are Via Christina, Nutcracker Exit, Marmolata Buttress, Sheerline, Bottomless Buttress and Boulder Ruckle Exit.

The park incorporates Durlston Head and its Great Globe, Anvil Point and a subterranean access problem in the form of Tilly Whim Caves which were closed through fear of accidents.

This five mile walk explores them all, and also brings in the superbly wild Dorset Naturalists' Trust reserve in the old Townsend Quarries above the south side of Swanage; though to find a suitable linking path we have to take you through caravans. The wardening at Durlston is low-profile but demanding, with plenty of problems happening at anti-social

---

hours, and on this walk there is much greater scope than usual for roaming at will. Take great care if the seabirds lure you to the cliffs. There is one notice at Durlston which you are asked to observe as a matter of course on this and any other walk: "Please leave the flowers for everyone to enjoy."

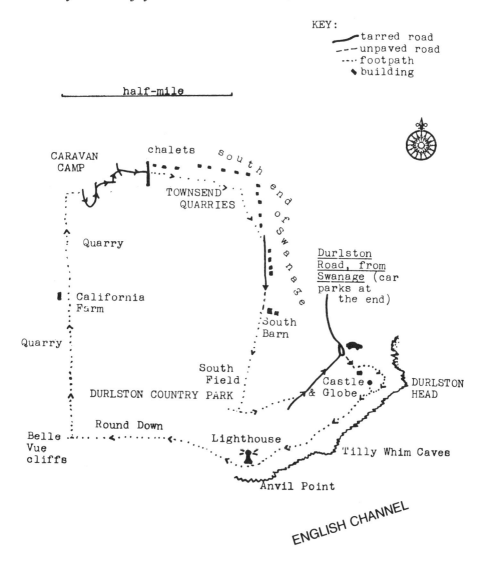

KEY:
—tarred road
---unpaved road
····footpath
❧ building

half-mile

• If you come into Swanage along the main road from Corfe Castle, the A351, you follow the "Durlston" signs which bring you into built-up Swanage through Kings Road West. You then pass the bus station and turn right at a mini-roundabout, into the main shopping centre. Turn right at the end of this street, into the main road along the back of the seafront — along which anyone from the Studland side of Purbeck will be coming towards Durlston. You then briefly follow the sea and turn right just before the Pier Head Restaurant, steeply uphill beside the Peveril open space. Half-way up the hill you turn left into Durlston Road and follow it all the way, through Swanage suburbia, on to the downs. You pass "15" mph markers and are inside Durlston Country Park. At the end of the road there is a turning circle with car-parks on both sides.

• Take the first, left-hand car park, if there are vacancies, (Ordnance Survey map reference SZ 033 773). The walk begins through its southern side, along a rough track with a notice: "Delivery vehicles only." It is signposted to the "Castle Cafe and Bar, Coast Path, Great Globe." You turn a corner to face the Durlston Head Castle, a large corbel-turreted restaurant set on the cliffs and surrounded by innumerable tablets of stone inscribed with statistics and poetry. It is a palatial French riviera-style villa of Purbeck stone, on land George Burt had bought in 1864. Three granite pillars were ordered by Sir Charles Barry for Trafalgar Square but turned out to be surplus and were inscribed by Burt: "Durlston Head Castle, above sea 215 feet."

• Take the second track downhill on the left, beside the castle wall. Keep turning right, to make a circuit of the headland. From it you look north into Durlston and Swanage Bays. The first bay has tumbled cliffs where the remains of some of the first marsupials have been found, from the beginning of the age of mammals. Old Harry Rocks are visible in the distance, and Bournemouth seafront beyond. Out to sea, on a clear day, is the tip of the Isle of Wight, at the Needles. At the end of the headlands is another of Burt's information stones: "Above sea 111 ft." Just around the corner you come to a flight of steps to the Great Globe. It weighs forty tons, is ten feet in diameter, and is carved in Portland stone, showing continents, oceans and rivers. It was made in sections at Mowlem's Greenwich works in 1887, and brought to Swanage in fifteen segments. It is "Above sea 136 ft." The information tablets behind it are dated 1891. At the same scale, we are told, "The Sun would be 1090 ft 0 ins" and "The Moon 2 feet 9 ins." The fastest object in our skies is named: "The common black swift flies at a rate of 200 miles per hour." On the other hand: "The Sun rotates once in 25 days: so a point on the solar equator is whirled round with a velocity of 4,500 miles an hour." "The distance from the Earth to the nearest fixed Star Alpha Centauri, visible in the southern hemisphere, is computed to be 200,000 times that of the Sun. Light which travels at the rate of about 186,000 miles a second would be three and a half years reaching the Earth from this Star." Enough, says Blaise Pascal: "Our nature consists in motion: perfect rest is death." Notice to the left of the exit a large scratched stone carved at the top: "Persons wishing to write their names will please do so on this stone only." Some have taken up the offer, and the tablets are not subjected to graffiti.

● Walk back down the steps on to the coastal path and turn right along it. A modern notice board gives you drawings of the "Birds of the sea-cliffs " and tells you to expect fulmars, kittiwakes, razorbills, guillemots, shags and herring gulls — which you will already have heard. The path westwards has its own poetry: "An iron coast and angry waves/ You seem to hear them rise and fall/ And roar rock — thwarted in their bellowing caves/ Beneath the windy wall. Above the sea 149 ft."

● You are approaching Anvil Point lighthouse. Before you reach it you pass the entrance to Tilly Whim Caves, which were closed at the time of writing because of rock-falls. Notice, however, the "1887" stone to the left of the entrance. These three octagonal pieces of granite stood beside Pentonville prison and were brought here when George Burt had this entrance into the old quarries blown out to provide a direct access into the caverns that avoided people having to stray on to another owner's land. Inside he added an inscription to the wall of the first gallery with a potted history: "These caves were formed centuries ago by men making sinks and rick-stones. Smuggling was also carried out here, and both were discontinued about the end of the French Wars, 1814." You next pass a steel tower with a triangle on top: the eastern of two sea-marks for a measured nautical mile, used in sea trials. From the lighthouse side of the valley you can look back into the two surviving openings of Tilly Whim and the collapsed end one. Tilly was a person and the "whim" a crane used to lower stones onto boats.

● Walk on the sea-side of the lighthouse. There is a modern notice to add to the Durlston collection. "The public are advised that a fog signal emitting a very loud noise may be sounded in this vicinity at any time without prior warning."

● From the lighthouse you turn fractionally inland, and climb to the top of the hill overlooking the coast. This is the hill immediately to the right of the cliffs. It is Round Down, though not so smooth now as it is heavily cratered by quarrying. At the centre are the foundations of a naval signal station of the Napoleonic period. It would have had a huge semaphore with shuttering in the shapes of squares and circles. At the end of the Round Down you cross a stone stile into the National Trust's Belle Vue cliffs.

● Then turn right, to head inland, and keep the stone wall on your right. You pass an active set of quarries, with stone ranging in size from great boulders down to the occasional piles of neatly-shaped blocks. Follow the footpath signs and walk at the bottom of the garden at California Farm. The farmer has a view down the valley to the Isle of Wight, which takes in the entire western coast to St Catherine's Point. On a clear morning he can lie in bed and tell the direction of the wind from the flares at Fawley oil refinery. Burt would be interested to know that the flares in the Gulf are the first man-made sight that this planet offers to astronauts returning from the moon — waste is something we can do so well.

● You descend into a caravan camp. On crossing its boundary

you turn immediately right, through a gap in the hedge, and then turn right again along the tarred road.

• Follow the drive as it swings leftwards, downhill, to pass the lavatory block. Turn right opposite caravan plot 39, and walk uphill passing numbers 54, 53 and 43A. Turn left opposite No. 47, downhill. You now have a view over Swanage and across to Ballard Down.

• Turn right at the crossroads between caravan plots 132 and 185. You then fork right, passing "car space 184", and caravans 173, 174, 178 and 179.

• Cross over the tarred road, half way up a hill, and follow the yellow "Footpath" marker on the other side. This corner of the nineteenth century Townsend Quarries does not have caravans, and is a nature reserve managed by Dorset Naturalists' Trust. Between the spoil heaps you pass an underground shaft, a grilled gap at the top of which provides a crucial refuge for bats of up to 17 species. The remains of stones a few yards from the entrance are its crabstones. These held a capstan, which was powered by a donkey on a circular path, to haul carts of stone from a hundred feet underground. There are a maze of paths between the thickets.

• The point you aim for is at the right-hand southern-upper-end of Swanage where the conifers start to outnumber the houses. The group of houses next to this part of the quarries have dormer windows.

• Here you come on to a tarred road and turn right along it, uphill. From the top of the ridge it becomes a stony track, straight ahead to a farmstead. Continue straight ahead from the South Barn, uphill through rough pastureland. After the next stone wall you are back in Durlston Country Park. This flat expanse was South Field, one of the three main areas of cultivation strips for medieval Swanage. Continue straight ahead, keeping the stone walls to your left. You come to a gate at the head of the valley overlooking the lighthouse.

• Turn left here, along the main grassy path to the lighthouse road. Turn left along the road, and follow it back to the car-parks.

Old Harry Rocks & Studland

Fifteen years after acquisition by the National Trust, the coastal chalklands of Ballard Down and Old Harry Rocks have been transformed from a reluctant prairie into recovering grassland. Their exposed position has ravaged hopes of full-scale cereal production. Nature is beginning to reassert herself and, though the full flora will take years to recover and perform again, improvements are visible everywhere across several hundred acres that have been rescued by the Trust from the Agricultural Revolution of the 1960s.

Commendably, through land agent Mark Harold, the National Trust has put the clock back to self-sufficient farming of the traditional sort. Permanent grass has been mixed with arable, cows with crops and measures taken to save Manor Farm at Studland from sinking into its own pool of slurry.

This five mile walk is a circuit of Ballard Down and Studland Manor Farm, bringing in the famous off-shore chalk stacks at the Pinnacle, Turf-Rick Rock and the great Old Harry collection that were, until recent times, the only pieces of land in these parts that the plough failed to reach.

An early casualty was the coast path, reduced in parts to virtually single-file width, but it has already widened into something of its former self as a swathe of well-trodden grass. Elsewhere, at the edges of the newly restored turf, there are clusters of tree tubes that will become plantations to supplement the decaying copses at Studland Wood and Warren Wood.

Overcoming problems with the landscape is proving easier than managing those of customer demand. Therefore, in an attempt to cheat the congestion at the heart of the holiday coast, this walk avoids the over-crowded and over-charged car parks of Studland and starts instead from the free and open space of an ordinary back-of-town layby on the northern outskirts of Swanage. Here, in the Ulwell Gap between two ridges of the Purbeck Hill, the scenery is superb with unploughable escarpments which are also mostly National Trust owned.

The route brings in a surfeit of history with the usual Dorset offering of prehistoric monuments being embellished by a bizarre collection of monumental bits of old London reassembled on these hills in celebration of the tapping of pure water from the chalk formation — which enabled the evolution of Swanage from a quarry port into an Edwardian spa.

In more recent times the local quarrying skills have revived Studiand's Saxon village cross and given it a new shaft that is a masterpiece of traditional style with a modern theme. Around these lanes, ex-guardsman Christopher Rone was the archetypal village bobby and was spotted by Enid Blyton who invariably spent her holidays in Swanage. She immortalised him as PC Plod in the Noddy stories.

Another literary aside is that the ashes of the novelist and futurist H G Wells were scattered in the sea off Old Harry Rocks in 1946 in response to a passage from his work that had been read at the memorial service: "We are all things that make the pass, striving upon a hidden mission, out to the open sea."

On land, you can venture a short distance down the lane beside Studland cross and find St Nicholas Church the oldest intact building in Dorset plus an overdose of memorials to interesting people and events.

Cornet Bankes, of the landowning family, was posthumously awarded the Victoria Cross for cheerfully accepting certain death in lighting the fuse that ended the siege of Lucknow in the Indian Mutiny. A military survivor with an international war record from South America and Spain and Waterloo was Sergeant William Lawrence who ended his days as landlord in the Bankes Arms. His gravestone is so wordy that it qualifies as a biography.

More poignant are the tragic inscriptions to the victims of shipwreck and weekend sailing misadventures in Studland Bay.

As for the church, of reddish brown gritty heathstone, it is notable as "one of only a dozen or so near-complete Norman village churches in England," to quote Fred Pitfield in *Purbeck Parish Churches*.

"Moreover the Norman work is built around the core of a still earlier pre-conquest structure, so that it can be regarded as the oldest surviving complete church in Dorset." In other words the shell is Saxon and — as Dorset has no intact castle or house earlier than fourteenth century Woodsford Castle — it is therefore the oldest complete building in the county.

So this is a walk with superlative history to match the breathtaking scenery.

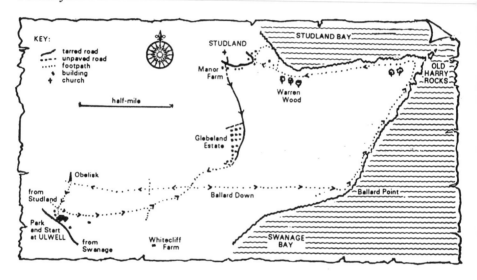

● Park at Ulwell, on the east side of the road just south of Godlingston Hill, in the large lay-by between Swanage Reservoir and Shepherds Farm (Ordnance Survey map reference SZ 021 809). There is a "Welcome to Swanage" sign set in a stone plinth.

● The walk starts at a kissing gate on the east side of the lay-by,

beside a gate and 15 yards from the Swanage sign. You cross a clear trickle of water and take the main path, uphill and just left of centre. Keep to the left-hand fence line and pass the "S W ACT 1883" inscription on a block of granite in 30 yards.

● This, and the obelisk of a former City of London gas-lamp on the hill-top, commemorate the

Swanage Water Act and the successful abstraction of pure water from the chalk aquifer.

● Seventy yards after the stone, just above the reservoir buildings, you come to a junction of paths with three options being signed on a marker stone.

● Turn right, following the arrow "To Coast Path". This takes you through the scrub at the foot of the Ballard Down escarpment. To the right there are glimpses of Swanage.

● In 150 yards you pass above a luxury home and follow the fence, keeping it to your right. There is now a reasonable view of Swanage Bay. At the end of this pasture the path crosses a stile to enter National Trust land at a "Ballard Down" sign. Continue straight ahead, towards the slanting hillside in the distance.

● In 350 yards, above Whitecliff Farm, you come to a hunting gate and a junction of paths. Turn left here, uphill and with your back to Swanage. There is a notice board and then a stone sign pointing to "Studland", followed by a couple of stone seats.

● Near the summit you come to a hunting gate and continue to the main fence-line which is on the brow of the hill in 70 yards. Here the view suddenly widens into a panorama of Poole Harbour, Bournemouth cliffs, Poole Bay and the Isle of Wight.

● Do not go through the gates but instead turn right, following the hilltop seaward along a path signed to "Old Harry Rocks and Coast Path". Continue along this path to the clifftop, in two thirds of a mile. You pass a pair of Bronze Age burial mounds, prehistoric cross-dykes and the remains of a wartime coastal radar station.

● The main track passes an Ordnance Survey triangulation pillar, at 383-feet on the cliffs, and then brings you to the coast path.

● Turn left along it, downhill and towards Old Harry Rocks, with the sea to your right.

● In another mile you are on the edge of Studland village. At the garden fence of the first building, with an attractive Victorian Gothic turret at the seaward corner, you continue straight ahead through the gate for the direct path into the village. The alternative is to turn right and enter Studland via the beach huts and sands and then turn left up the South Beach track.

• Either way you emerge on a lane, beside the public toilets. Turn left here, passing thatched cottages numbers 2 and 3, and walk up to the 1976 "Spaceship Earth" cross by Purbeck marbler Treleven Haysom which is set on a Saxon plinth at the junction of the road leading to St Nicholas Church.

• Facing the cross is the Dairy House of Manor Farm. Turn left beside it, along the track between the farmhouse and its outbuildings, which is signed from the crossroads as a "Public Footpath to Ballard Down and Swanage".

• It takes you via the hillside Glebeland Estate in half a mile. Thirty yards after the last house, Summer Hill, you turn left through a gateway beside an electricity pole. "Swanage 1½", the path is signed.

• On top of Ballard Down there is a stone seat inscribed "REST AND BE THANKFULL" (sic) and "D J 1852" for brilliant Victorian law-writer David Jardine who adopted Swanage.

• Go through the gate and turn sharp right, following the fence along the ridge of the hill with an expansive view in both directions. Keep going straight ahead.

• In the dip in just over half a mile you come to the commemorative obelisk, set on a Bronze Age burial mound. The original inscription records the fact that the Cornish granite was "taken down from near the Mansion House, London, and re-erected here in 1892". Note the evidence of its intended purpose at the centre of the displaced hexagonal column, once the lower section of the obelisk, viz the gas-pipe. A plaque gives the more recent history, of demolition "in 1941 to avoid its being of assistance to enemy aircraft during the war" and re-erection in 1973 by the Royal Engineers.

• Turn left at the obelisk, over the stile, and head downhill to Ulwell. There is a caravan camp in the middle distance with Swanage Brickworks behind.

• The path follows a fence down the steep slope and you turn left on reaching the yew trees at the bottom. Keep the trees and the reservoir buildings to your right.

• In a hundred yards you are back at the lay-by and your car.